THIS WALKER BOOK BELONGS TO:

_____

_____

_____

_____

For
Sebastian
with love

First published 1992 by
Walker Books Ltd, 87 Vauxhall Walk
London SE11 5HJ

This edition published 1995

4 6 8 10 9 7 5 3

© 1992 Helen Craig

This book has been typeset in Garamond.

Printed in Hong Kong

British Library Cataloguing in Publication Data
A catalogue record for this book is
available from the British Library.

ISBN 0-7445-3151-9

THE TOWN MOUSE AND THE COUNTRY MOUSE

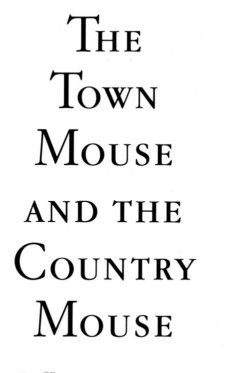

Retold and Illustrated by HELEN CRAIG

WALKER BOOKS
AND SUBSIDIARIES

LONDON • BOSTON • SYDNEY

Once upon a time, deep in the hedgerow, there lived a country mouse called Charlie. One afternoon, he was sitting at his window listening to a blackbird singing while the sun warmed the fur on his back, when suddenly there was a knock at the door. It was his cousin, Tyler the town mouse.

"Hello there, Charlie! I've come to visit," said Tyler, marching in and flopping down in Charlie's best armchair. "I'm exhausted. What a journey! Got anything to eat?"

Charlie fetched him a bowl of nuts and marigold seeds topped with some red hawthorn berries he had been saving for a special treat. But Tyler wrinkled his nose. "What plain food," he said. "Still, I suppose it's good for you."

When he had finished eating, he leant back. "Now, Charlie, is there anything going on around here in the evenings?" Charlie smiled. "Yes, there is. I'll take you to see something wonderful."

That evening they
climbed the hill behind
Charlie's house.
The sun was just going
down and all the birds
were singing their best
songs. They waited
while the sky filled with
brilliant colours.
"There!" whispered Charlie.
"Where?" said Tyler.

"The sunset," said Charlie.
"Isn't it beautiful?"
Tyler yawned. "Too slow
for me. I like a bit of action."
And he set off down the hill.

That night, Tyler couldn't sleep. The countryside was just too dark and quiet.

Next morning, when he saw that breakfast was nuts, seeds and berries again, he decided enough was enough.

"Sorry, Charlie," he said. "Country life is not for me. I need the bright lights of the town. But why don't you come back with me and see how exciting life can be?"

Charlie had never been further than the top of the hill, but he said bravely, "All right, I will. Just let me pack a few things." And they set off.

They had not gone far when they met a carrier pigeon. "I'm on my way to town," she said. "Would you like a lift? Climb aboard and hold on tight!"

To TOWN 10 MILES

As they soared high into the air, Charlie watched his hedgerow get smaller and smaller until it disappeared. He felt quite lost.

It was a long journey. At last the carrier pigeon set them down in the town market-place. Charlie stood rooted to the spot. There were so many people; there was so much noise.

"Come on, Charlie," hissed Tyler, dragging him into the safety of the shadows.

"It's dangerous here. Stick close and follow me."

They scuttled off, along a gutter,

across a pavement,

up an iron staircase,

over rooftops,

down a chimney,

and through a window.

At the end of a musty
passage, bright light
streamed from a small hole.

"In we go," whispered Tyler
and he squeezed through.
Charlie followed.

Aaaah! A giant cat with fierce eyes and huge sharp teeth
was waiting to pounce on them! **"Help!"** squealed Charlie.

He swayed and fell, but Tyler caught him by the tail. He was laughing. "Don't be silly, Charlie, we're in a cinema. It's only a film."

Poor Charlie peeped through his paws. The giant cat was now chasing a giant mouse. It was all very strange.

The film ended and
they set off again
through the dark streets.
On the way Charlie
nearly got squashed…

gassed…

drowned in a
sea of paper…

and knocked out by
a runaway pineapple.

"You must be more careful!"
said Tyler, picking him up
for the fourth time.

Charlie was very glad when
they reached the steps of the
big house where Tyler lived.

"I expect you're hungry," said Tyler leading the way to the dining-room. "Let's see what's left." And he dashed round the table looking for the best bits. "Have some sardines and chocolate mousse," he said.

"How about prawns in mayonnaise or prunes and custard?"

He offered Charlie sausages,
ice-cream and a bit of
fatty bacon.

"Have a drink!" he called,
knocking over a wine glass.
Charlie didn't like any of
it much. He was beginning
to feel very sick and dizzy.

Suddenly there
was a horrible
noise.
Yeowwoull!
Thump!
Crash!
A fat cat landed
on the table.
Tyler vanished.

The cat sprang.
Charlie jumped.

The cat chased
him round and
round and up
and down,

until Charlie
dived under a
sofa and scuttled
up into one of
the springs.

The cat could smell Charlie.
Charlie could smell the cat.
The cat watched the sofa for a
long, long time. Charlie waited,
trembling. He thought his
end had come and he would
never see his comfortable
home in the hedgerow again.

At last he heard the cat being shooed out and almost at once Tyler appeared.

"Sorry, Charlie. Forgot to tell you where the mouse hole was. Are you all right? You look a bit odd."

And he led Charlie to his home under the sideboard and put him to bed.

Charlie had nightmares all night.

Very early in the
morning he woke
Tyler and said,
"I'm sorry, town life
is just too much
for me. I think I'd
better go home."

So Tyler took him
back to the market-
place and put him
on a milk van that
was going to the farm
near the hedgerow.

Charlie was so pleased
to be home again. He
ate a large dish of red
hawthorn berries while
the blackbird sang and
the sun warmed the
fur on his back.

That night Tyler put on his top hat, white tie and tails and set off across town for some fun at the theatre. He was very happy.

Under the same night sky, Charlie lay on his hill. He had watched the sun set and now he was counting the stars. He was very happy too!

MORE WALKER PAPERBACKS
For You to Enjoy

THIS IS THE BEAR

by Sarah Hayes / Helen Craig

Three rollicking cumulative rhymes about the adventures of a boy, a dog and a bear.

"For those ready for their first story, there could be no better choice…
Helen Craig's pictures are just right." *Judy Taylor, The Independent*

0-7445-0969-6   *This Is the Bear*
0-7445-1304-9   *This Is the Bear and the Picnic Lunch*
0-7445-3147-0   *This Is the Bear and the Scary Night*
£4.50 each

THE ONE AND ONLY ROBIN HOOD

by Nigel Gray / Helen Craig

A very merry retelling of a popular tale with a lively question and answer format,
speech bubbles, delightful pictures and elements from the well-known rhymes
"Sing a Song of Sixpence" and "Diddle, Diddle, Dumpling, My Son John".

"Very enjoyable, original and with cheerful, busy illustrations,
appealing to a wide age-range." *Books for Keeps*

0-7445-1424-X   £3.99

THE YELLOW HOUSE

by Blake Morrison / Helen Craig

Every day a little girl passes the mysterious yellow house, wondering who lives there.
Then one day a little boy invites her in…

"A magical fantasy… Full of delight and surprise." *Children's Books of the Year*

0-7445-1361-8   £2.99

Walker Paperbacks are available from most booksellers, or by post from B.B.C.S., P.O. Box 941, Hull, North Humberside HU1 3YQ

24 hour telephone credit card line 01482 224626

To order, send: Title, author, ISBN number and price for each book ordered, your full name and address,
cheque or postal order payable to BBCS for the total amount and allow the following for postage and packing:
UK and BFPO: £1.00 for the first book, and 50p for each additional book to a maximum of £3.50.
Overseas and Eire: £2.00 for the first book, £1.00 for the second and 50p for each additional book.

Prices and availability are subject to change without notice.